Pearson

GW01271357

Year 5

Grammar and Punctuation
Activity Workbook

Author:
Hannah
Hirst-Dunton

Published by Pearson Education Limited, 80 Strand, London, WC2R 0RL.
www.pearsonschools.co.uk

Text © Pearson Education Limited 2022
Edited by Florence Production Ltd
Designed by Pearson Education Limited 2022
Typeset by Florence Production Ltd
Produced by Florence Production Ltd and Sarah Loader
Original illustrations © Pearson Education Limited 2022
Cover design by Pearson Education Limited 2022

The right of Hannah Hirst-Dunton to be identified as author of this work has been asserted by her in
accordance with the Copyright, Designs and Patents Act 1988.

First published 2022

25 24 23 22
10 9 8 7 6 5 4 3 2 1

British Library Cataloguing in Publication Data
A catalogue record for this book is available from the British Library

ISBN 978 1 292 42501 6

Printed in Slovakia by Neografia

Acknowledgements
Front Cover: AnnstasAg/Shutterstock
Design: © Pearson Education Limited, 2021

The author and publisher would like to thank the following individuals and organisations for permission
to reproduce photographs:

(Key: b-bottom; c-centre; l-left; r-right; t-top)

Shutterstock: Olga Utchenko iv, 10, 22, 32, 49, 62; Spreadthedesign iv, 10, 22, 32, 49, 62; Tegah Mujiono
iv, 10, 22, 32, 49, 62; AnnstasAg/Shutterstock 81bc, 82bc

All other images © Pearson Education Limited

Notes from the publisher
Pearson has robust editorial processes, including answer and fact checks, to ensure the accuracy of the
content in this publication, and every effort is made to ensure this publication is free of errors. We are,
however, only human, and occasionally errors do occur. Pearson is not liable for any misunderstandings
that arise as a result of errors in this publication, but it is our priority to ensure that the content is
accurate. If you spot an error, please do contact us at resourcescorrections@pearson.com so we can
make sure it is corrected.

Contents

About this book

This book will help your child to improve their basic literacy skills, fill gaps in learning and increase confidence in a fun and engaging way. It offers a simple, approachable way for you to guide your child through the grammar and punctuation requirements of the National Curriculum.

Your child's mastery of grammar will allow them to express themselves clearly and meet expectations within the whole English curriculum, and beyond!

Grammar and punctuation made clear

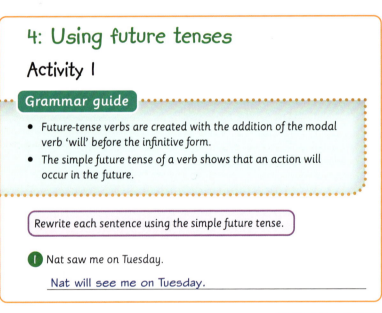

- This activity book is split into bite-sized, manageable topics that are clearly named.
- Each topic is broken down into a number of sessions that develop particular skills and understanding.
- Every session includes grammar or punctuation guides, which give 'at a glance' guidance.

- Then three activities introduce, practise and reinforce the skill focus.
- Completing all three activities in one sitting will help your child get to grips with the concept.
- There are checkpoints for your child to fill in at the end of each topic. This gives you the chance to see where further support is needed.

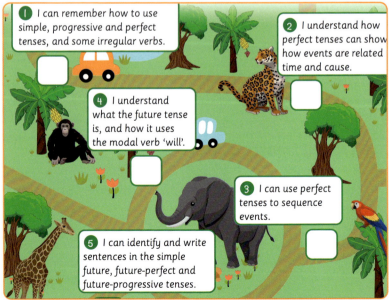

How to use this book

- Short sessions work best. Try setting aside half an hour for your child to explore the three activities.

- Try to complete the topics in the given order, as many of them form key foundations for the ones that follow.

- Your child will ideally work through topics independently, but it's worth being there for when support is needed.

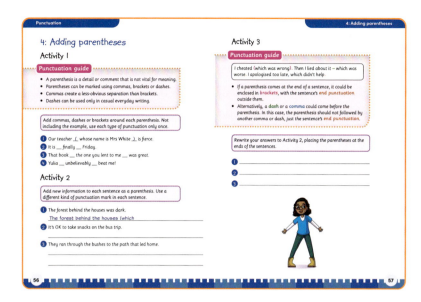

- If your child seems bored or is struggling, suggest they take a break. It might be that they understand the ideas already, or just need time to take something in. They could work on a creative task, such as colouring or following patterns. Try the Pearson Handwriting Activity Workbooks: they contain lots of fun activities, and will also help your child to practise pencil control.

- At the end of a topic, explore the checkpoints with your child and make sure you're happy with what they've understood.

Building from ...

These topics follow on directly from Year 4 to Year 5:

Year 4 topic	Year 5 topic
Revising determiners and pronouns	Demonstratives
Verb forms for Standard English	Verb forms
More expanded noun phrases	Relative clauses
Fronted adverbials	Exploring adverbials
Punctuation	Punctuation

Building towards ...

These topics lead on directly from Year 5 to Year 6:

Year 5 topic	Year 6 topic
Exploring adverbials	Adjectives, adverbials and prepositions
Verb forms	Further verb forms
Relative clauses	Formal and informal registers
Punctuation	Punctuation

Getting started

- Make your child's learning space interesting and fun, in a favourite place to sit or with a favourite toy beside them.
- Encourage your child to step away from any technology or energetic games a little while beforehand, and to take some deep breaths to help them focus.
- Make sure they're sitting comfortably at a table and holding their pencil properly.
- Try to sit with your child to start, even if you're occupied with your own task.

A helping hand

Remind your child to ask for help when they need it. In some topics, you may find they need a little extra guidance. Follow the tips below to support them.

Relative clauses: What are relative clauses? (pages 35 to 36)

Understanding the difference between definitive and incidental information is important for future topics. Read the Grammar guide on page 35 with your child. Then alter the example to suit your environment in different contexts.

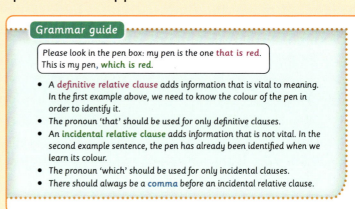

Grammar guide

Please look in the pen box: my pen is the one that is red. This is my pen, which is red.

- A definitive relative clause adds information that is vital to meaning. In the first example above, we need to know the colour of the pen in order to identify it.
- The pronoun 'that' should be used for only definitive clauses.
- An incidental relative clause adds information that is not vital. In the second example sentence, the pen has already been identified when we learn its colour.
- The pronoun 'which' should be used for only incidental clauses.
- There should always be a comma before an incidental relative clause.

For example, while cooking you could ask your child to find just 'the bowl' (which is unclear) and then 'the bowl that is on the top shelf'. Note that the extra information defines which bowl you want: it is 'definitive' information. Make an extra observation about the bowl, such as 'You found the bowl, which we'll use to beat the eggs.' Embed the terminology by noting that you added an 'incidental' detail: an unnecessary one.

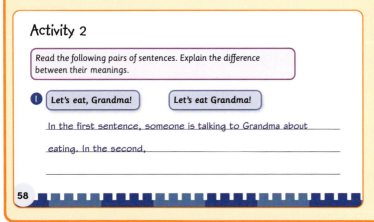

Activity 2

Read the following pairs of sentences. Explain the difference between their meanings.

1 Let's eat, Grandma!   Let's eat Grandma!

In the first sentence, someone is talking to Grandma about eating. In the second,

58

Punctuation: How can commas help with clarity? (pages 58 to 59) and Using commas for clarity (pages 60 to 61)

Your child may find it both fun and helpful to say the sentences aloud and discuss them. Suggest that they use these given sentences as models for writing their own.

Tricky concepts

Choosing 'which' or 'that'

Many people, in writing as well as in everyday speech, use 'which' and 'that' interchangeably. This is one of the instances in which formal grammar and everyday use aren't quite in step! In formal grammar, there are definite rules for which to choose: they tie in with the concept of 'incidental' information. As children may have difficulty with this, **Relative clauses** is a topic that's drawn out as one with which children may need a 'helping hand'.

Modal verbs

We use the future tense all the time, but modal verbs can still be tricky. You could focus on 'will' for longer, embedding understanding of how it affects meaning, before moving on to the other modal verbs.

Technical terms

Even when children know and understand the structures of grammar, terminology can make things seem difficult. Help your child to use the Glossary, which makes the terms clearer.

Progress check

- Once your child has worked on some activities, judge how confident they are with carrying on alone. If they're keen for independence, they're probably on the right track.
- Encourage your child to talk to you about what they are learning. Getting an explanation in their own words will show you how much they've understood.

Extension activities

- To extend practice of definitive and incidental clauses, challenge your child to reverse the activity suggested as a helping hand above, asking you to find something. Challenge them to use the correct terminology to explain what they're doing at each point.
- As in Year 4, challenge your child to apply their skills with cohesion and paragraph structure in longer pieces of writing. Set topics you feel your child will enjoy exploring, or ones that tie in with their other composition activities.

Putting grammar and punctuation skills to use

Help your child to understand that their new grammar and punctuation skills are in use everywhere. Encourage them to find examples around them, including in their reading materials.

- When your child is reading longer narratives, ask them to spot past-perfect and present-perfect verbs that are being used to show how events link together.
- Ask your child to listen for demonstratives in spoken language and playscripts, where they will be more common than in other writing.

1: Revising fronted adverbials

Activity 1

Grammar guide

> We're **quite hurriedly** on the way to meet Mel.
> **Next**, we'll **probably** go to the park.

- An **adverbial** is a word or phrase that can add information about a verb, an adjective or another adverb.
- A **fronted adverbial** is put at the start of a sentence, followed by a **comma**.
- **Fronted adverbials** can be used to link ideas. '**Next**' links the sentences by showing how one event will lead to another in time.

Underline the fronted adverbial in each pair of sentences.

1. Ana walked up the hill. <u>At the top</u>, there would be a wonderful view.
2. Ji shut his eyes, sighed and began counting. After reaching ten, he looked up.
3. Will you be walking home from school? If so, please would you go to the shop?
4. Kerry could not swim. However, she planned to learn.

Activity 2

Grammar guide

- Adverbials can add information about any of the following things:

  - time (such as 'then')
  - manner (such as 'loudly')
  - cause (such as 'due to snow')
  - probability (such as 'perhaps')
  - place (such as 'nearby')
  - degree (such as 'not very')
  - number (such as 'once')
  - frequency (such as 'annually')

- Links can also be made in these ways.

Underline the fronted adverbial in each pair. Draw lines to match the sentences to the kind of link that is made.

1 a Finish your homework. <u>After that,</u> you can go out.

b Kay lives at number 23. Next door, there's a gym.

c I woke up early. As a result, I took my time eating breakfast.

place

cause

time

2 a It's easy to make cupcakes. Firstly, weigh out the flour.

b We usually have fish on Fridays. Sometimes, that varies.

c Winning isn't vital. More than that, we need team spirit.

degree

number

frequency

Activity 3

Circle each fronted adverbial and add a label to show the kind of link it makes.

number

Dear Diary – I started at the new school today. Firstly, I had to go to registration and I thought I'd really stand out. When I got there, I saw there were lots of new pupils. Consequently, I calmed down a bit! Nervously, I started talking to the others. Just possibly, I'll make some friends!

2: Linking sentences with fronted adverbials

Activity 1

Grammar guide

- Fronted adverbials can be used to link sentences.

Look at the pairs of sentences. Draw a line to match each pair to the adverbial that would be most suitable for linking them.

1. I ate my breakfast. I took a walk in the park.

2. I thought I'd forgotten my sports kit. It was still in my bag.

3. I did brilliantly in the maths test. I won ten house points.

4. The forest was huge. There was a small cottage.

5. The first task was reading the story. We had to answer the questions about it.

As a result,

Secondly,

Later that morning,

Fortunately, though,

At its edge,

Activity 2

Grammar guide

- Adverbials can create links related to any of the following things.
  - time
  - place
  - manner
  - degree
  - cause
  - number
  - probability
  - frequency

Look at the sentences below. Add a fronted adverbial to the second sentence in each pair, creating different kinds of links.

1 Create a **time** link.

We had a science lesson. ___Afterwards___, we had a PE lesson.

2 Create a **place** link.

The path was long. _____, there was a bench.

3 Create a **cause** link.

Mari was about to go on holiday. _____, she packed her case.

4 Create a **frequency** link.

I wash my hair twice a week. _____, I clean my teeth.

5 Create a **degree** link.

I don't like dancing very much. _____, I enjoy singing.

Activity 3

Write three sentences about things you did at the weekend.
Use two fronted adverbials that link the sentences in different ways.
Label them to show what kinds of information they add.

_____

_____

_____

3: How can fronted adverbials add structure?

Activity 1

Grammar guide

Initially, it is important to understand a skill. Studying how others use it will help you to learn. Think about how to apply their methods in future.

Later, you can start to experiment for yourself, remembering what you learned.

- If a piece of writing has cohesion, the sentences in it are linked together to become effective as a whole.
- **Fronted adverbials** can add cohesion between paragraphs.
- They can signal the structure of a text clearly for the reader.
- The fronted adverbial at the start of a paragraph should apply to the whole paragraph.

Look at these paragraphs. Underline each fronted adverbial.

Many children believe that school uniform is a bad idea, and want to wear their own clothes to lessons. They say that it helps them to relax.

<u>However</u>, I believe there are benefits to having a uniform. It has an important part to play in school life, in more than one way.

Firstly, it suggests belonging and a united school. Pupils are clearly linked to each other and to the school itself. This can help to improve behaviour, as pupils become school representatives.

Secondly, it prepares pupils for the fact that they may need separate work clothes in the future.

Most importantly, it prevents competition between pupils. Fashion can divide opinions strongly.

Activity 2

Look at the instructions for changing batteries in a remote control. Note that the fronted adverbials mark new paragraphs.
To show the order in which they make sense, number the paragraphs 1 to 5 and label the sentences in each paragraph using the letters a, b and c.
Paragraphs may contain one, two or three sentences.

1 **b** You will also need a small cross-head screwdriver.	Finally, insert the new batteries into the remote control.	Squeeze the yellow clip to open the panel when you have removed the screws.
Firstly, open the battery panel by removing the two screws.	**1** **a** Before you begin, make sure you have the correct kind of batteries.	The panel is hinged and will open upwards.
Dispose of the old batteries safely.	Next, lift out the old batteries.	When you have your equipment, lay the remote control upside down.

Activity 3

Look at the fronted adverbials you underlined in Activity 1.
What purposes do they have in the text? Write your ideas.

_____

_____

_____

4: Using fronted adverbials for structure

Activity 1

Grammar guide

- If a piece of writing has cohesion, the sentences in it are linked together to become effective as a whole.
- Fronted adverbials can add cohesion between paragraphs. They can help to signal the structure of a text clearly for the reader.
- The fronted adverbial at the start of a paragraph should apply to the whole paragraph.
- New paragraphs are needed when any of the following things change.
  - ○ topic
  - ○ time
  - ○ setting
  - ○ speaker

Look at the text, noting the fronted adverbials.
Mark the text where you would start each new paragraph.

Mo awoke very early that morning. The sun was just about to rise, and the birds were singing. He knew no one else would be up yet. After lying in bed for ten minutes, he decided to get up. He stretched and pulled on his slippers before leaving his bedroom. Downstairs, Mo wandered into the kitchen. He had decided to make himself breakfast and watch the sun come up. He enjoyed having such peace and quiet around him, and he took his time. All of a sudden, there was a noise from the garden. The sound rang out loudly in the still morning air. Running to the door, Mo looked out. He laughed at his panic: there was a startled-looking cat next to the dustbin's fallen lid.

Activity 2

Add adverbials to this text. Use them to add different kinds of information, and to link both paragraphs and sentences.

Long ago _____, there lived a strange young woman. She could sing, she could dance and she could, _____, tell tall tales. _____, she had no family. _____, she had always lived entirely alone.

*

_____, the young woman came up with a plan to end her loneliness. _____, she needed to ensure she was familiar with every possible route to her home. She explored _____.

*

_____, she would practise her talents. _____, she would sing, dance and tell her stories.

*

_____, she was ready to put her plan into action.

Activity 3

Think about other adverbials that you could have chosen to complete Activity 2. If you would like to change any of your choices, write them down.

_____

_____

_____

What do I Know?

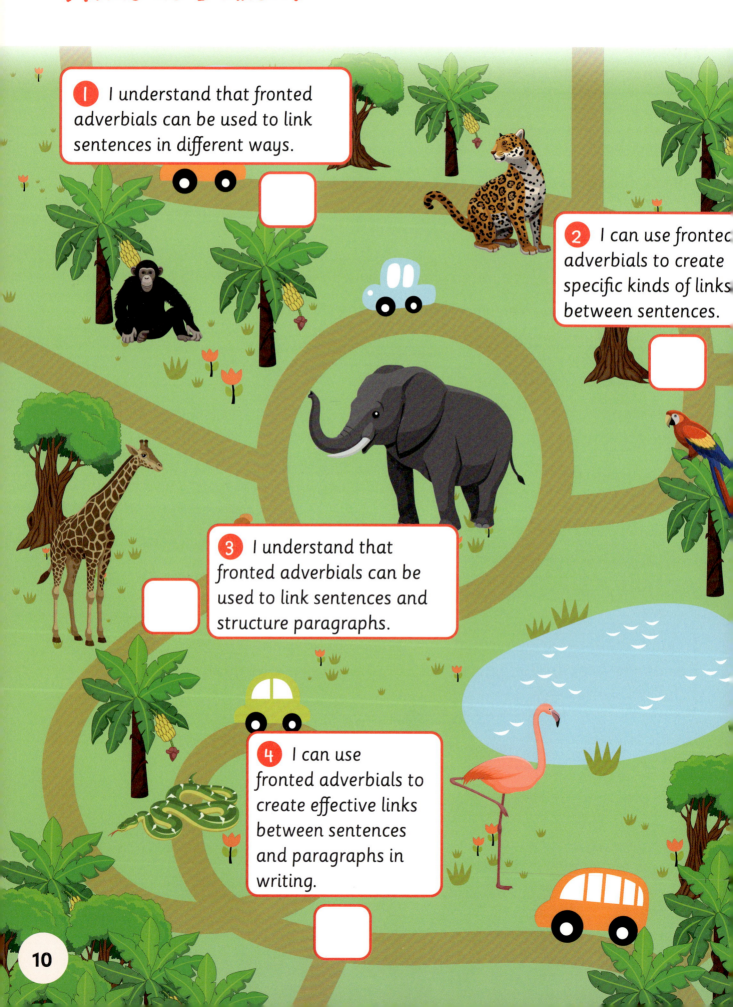

1 I understand that fronted adverbials can be used to link sentences in different ways.

2 I can use fronted adverbials to create specific kinds of links between sentences.

3 I understand that fronted adverbials can be used to link sentences and structure paragraphs.

4 I can use fronted adverbials to create effective links between sentences and paragraphs in writing.

1: Remembering tenses

Activity 1

Grammar guide

> I look. I looked. I am looking. I was looking. I have looked.
> I had looked.
> She looks. She looked. She is looking. She was looking.
> She has looked. She had looked.
> They look. They looked. They are looking. They were looking.
> They have looked. They had looked.

- Verbs can be formed in different ways, to suit their tense (when the actions happen) and their person (who or what does the action).
- The ways they change also depend on the way the end of the verb is formed.
- Some past tenses, and the present tense of 'be', are irregular. These just have to be learned.
- Tenses that should be familiar are the simple present, simple past, present progressive, past progressive, present perfect and past perfect.

Write the tense of each pair of sentences.

1. We are arriving and I am enjoying the show. The acrobat is dashing and flying. _____

2. We have arrived and I have enjoyed the show. The acrobat has dashed and flown. _____

3. We arrive and I enjoy the show. The acrobat dashes and flies. _____

4. We had arrived and I had enjoyed the show. The acrobat had dashed and flown. _____

5. We arrived and I enjoyed the show. The acrobat dashed and flew. _____

6. We were arriving and I was enjoying the show. The acrobat was dashing and flying. _____

Activity 2

Complete this table with the correct verb forms for the third-person present: verb forms that should follow the pronoun 'she', 'he' or 'it'.

Infinitive	Simple present	Simple past	Present progressive	Past progressive	Present perfect	Past perfect
1. to want						
2. to watch						
3. to spy						
4. to grow						
5. to be						
6. to have						

Activity 3

Write six short sentences, each containing one of the verbs above. Use a different tense in each sentence.

_____

_____

_____

_____

_____

_____

2: Perfect verbs for effect

Activity 1

Grammar guide

> Gregor **had planned** to visit us, but he **missed** the train.
>
> He **has missed** the train so he **phones** me.

- Perfect verbs can help to show the order in which events occur.
- **Past perfect verbs** show that events had effects on **later events in the past**.
- **Present perfect verbs** show that events have effects on the **present**.

Each pair of sentences describes three events.
Note down the order in which these events occurred,
according to what the verbs tell you.

---

1 Maya had been out in the rain but then she went home.
She has gone home so now she is dry.

___being out in the rain___   _____

_____

2 I'm relieved because I have taken my singing exam.
I had practised just before it.

_____   _____

_____

Activity 2

Complete each sentence with the most suitable form of the verb shown in brackets: present perfect or past perfect.

1 Aaron ___has lived___ here since March. (to live)

2 I _____ all the way, but I was still late. (to run)

3 Karen knew her sister _____ her cardigan. (to take)

4 Leroy is so proud that he _____ the prize. (to win)

5 Your mother _____ to stay, so we have (to choose)
to wait.

Activity 3

Write one or two sentences that show the numbered order of events. Use one past-perfect verb, one present-perfect verb and one present-tense verb. A full example answer has been given to help you.

| 1. Buying eggs | 2. Breaking them | 3. Needing more |

I had bought eggs but I have broken them and now I need more.

_____

| 1. Feeling unwell | 2. Taking the day off | 3. Feeling better |

_____

_____

3: What are future tenses?

Activity 1

Grammar guide

> I **will** **walk**. You **will** **walk**. She **will** **walk**. We **will** **walk**. They **will** **walk**.

- The simple future tense of a verb shows that an action will happen in the future.
- Future-tense verbs are created with the addition of 'will' before the **infinitive** form.
- The word 'will' is a modal verb.

Tick the sentences that are in the future tense. Underline the modal verb in each ticked sentence.

- I <u>will</u> be at home on Thursday evening. ✓
- Georgia wants to see you after dinner. ☐
- Mr Tirenz will do what he can to help you. ☐
- They will look out for the helicopter. ☐
- We haven't seen each other for months. ☐

Activity 2

Grammar guide

> You **will** **have** left by the time I arrive.
> You **will** **be** leaving by the time I arrive.

- **Future-perfect** and **future-progressive** tenses use both <u>modal verbs</u> and <u>auxiliary verbs</u>.
- The **future-perfect** tense expresses that something will be perfectly completed at a point in the future. The modal verb and auxiliary verb are always in the form 'will have'.
- The **future-progressive** tense expresses that something will continue over a period of time in the future. The modal verb and auxiliary verb are always in the form 'will be'.

Tick the sentences that use future tense verbs correctly. Underline the mistakes in the other sentences.

- I will see you at school. ✓
- Your brother <u>be</u> waiting for you at the bus stop. ☐
- Roni will really happy to get home. ☐
- We will have looked everywhere for these keys. ☐
- It will be raining all weekend. ☐
- The horse will had been in training for a whole year. ☐

Activity 3

Draw lines to label each sentence with its tense.

1. Ms Sunitri will be running in a race.   simple future
2. The road will soon be flooded.   future perfect
3. No time will have been wasted.   future progressive

4: Using future tenses

Activity 1

Grammar guide

- Future-tense verbs are created with the addition of the modal verb 'will' before the infinitive form.
- The simple future tense of a verb shows that an action will occur in the future.

> Rewrite each sentence using the simple future tense.

1 Nat saw me on Tuesday.

Nat will see me on Tuesday.

2 Daka and her sister go home.

_____

3 Uri sang along with the radio.

_____

Activity 2

Grammar guide

- The future-perfect tense expresses that something will be perfectly completed at a point in the future.
- The future-progressive tense expresses that something will continue over a period of time in the future.
- Future-perfect and future-progressive tenses use modal verbs and auxiliary verbs.

Rewrite the following passage using the future tense.

Ideally, you brought these instructions so you were able to find your way. You had caught the 11:30 bus from town. You were getting off the bus when you saw the small park to the left. There was a bright red postbox straight ahead. You took the path by the postbox and there, to your right, was my house.

Ideally, you will bring _____

_____

_____

_____

_____

_____

_____

Activity 3

Change these irregular past-tense verbs to their future tenses.

1 began   _____

2 told   _____

3 fell   _____

4 thought   _____

5: How are other modal verbs used?

Activity 1

Grammar guide

I **can** go. I **could** go. I **may** go. I **might** go. I **should** go. I **would** go.
I **must** go. I <u>have to</u> go. I <u>need to</u> go. I <u>ought to</u> go.

- The verb 'will' is not the only modal verb.
- **Other modal verbs** also come before the **main verb's infinitive form**.
- Like 'will', other modal verbs do not change in form.
- <u>Some modal verbs include the word 'to'.</u>

Tick the sentences that use modal verbs.
Underline the modal verb in each ticked sentence.

- It <u>should</u> be easy for Mum to fix the blender. ☑
- I can come and collect the parcel after school. ☐
- We definitely need some help with this. ☐
- Daren's brother was getting fed up of his laziness. ☐
- You have to get the train at 9:15. ☐
- Could Jin-Yang come with us? ☐

Activity 2

Grammar guide

- Modal verbs can show how likely or how important the verb's action is.
- Modal verbs apart from 'will' show that the action may or may not happen.
- The modal verb 'will' shows that something is certain to happen, but not how important it is.

Draw lines to show how likely it is that the action will happen.

1	I should do it.	most likely
2	I will do it.	second most likely
3	I must do it.	third most likely
4	I could do it.	least likely

Activity 3

Grammar guide

I **can** swim. You **may** begin eating. He **should** help out more.

- Modal verbs can express different things, such as **ability** (if something is possible), **permission** (if something is allowed) or **obligation** (if something is a duty).

Draw lines to show what kind of information each modal verb gives.

1	ought to	ability
2	may	permission
3	could	obligation

6: Expressing probability

Activity 1

Grammar guide

I **could leave** now. I **will leave** now.

- **Modal verbs** come before the **main verb's infinitive form**.
- Their form does not change.
- They can show how probable or how important the verb's action is.
- The modal verb 'will' always shows the most probable actions. It indicates that something is certain to happen, but not how important it is.

Choose one of the modal verbs below to complete each sentence. Use each modal verb only once.

| must | ought to | could | would |

1 It's possible that I _____could_____ come to visit you.

2 I _____ have helped if I'd been able to.

3 I _____ be finishing my homework instead of playing.

4 My aunt says I _____ tidy my room.

Activity 2

Write the start of a story in which you are the main character. Include all of the activities below. Use different modal verbs to express how important it is that you do each activity.

doing homework

seeing friends

practising sport

eating dinner

_____

_____

_____

_____

_____

Activity 3

Look again at your response to Activity 2. Write the actions in the order of importance.

Most important:	
Second most important:	
Third most important:	
Least important:	

What do I know?

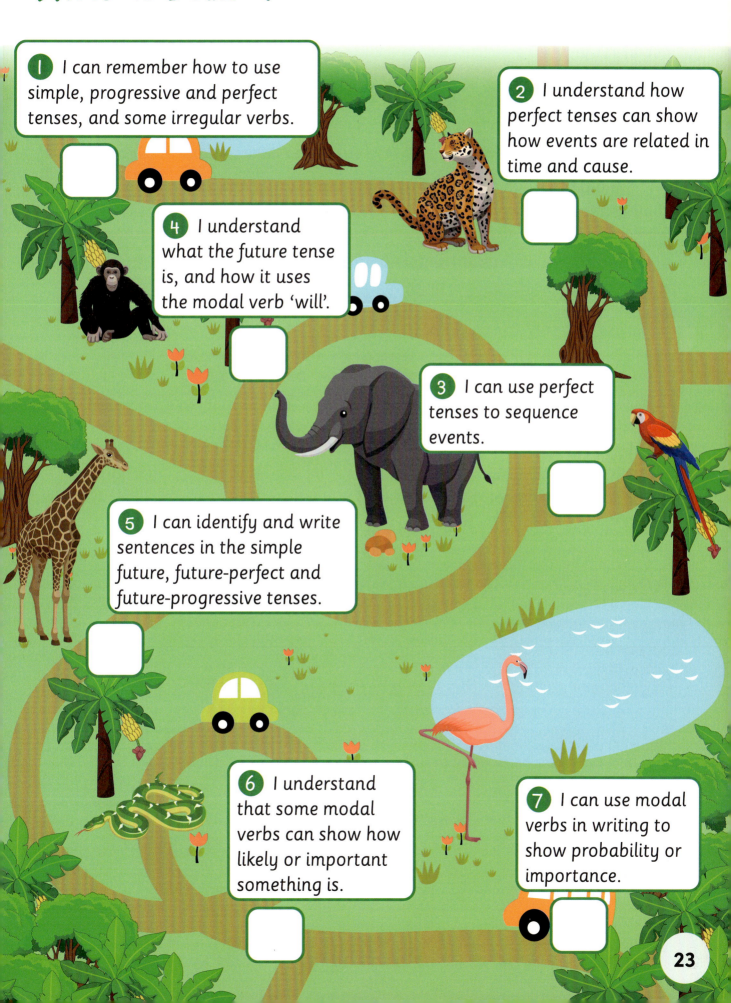

1 I can remember how to use simple, progressive and perfect tenses, and some irregular verbs.

2 I understand how perfect tenses can show how events are related in time and cause.

4 I understand what the future tense is, and how it uses the modal verb 'will'.

3 I can use perfect tenses to sequence events.

5 I can identify and write sentences in the simple future, future-perfect and future-progressive tenses.

6 I understand that some modal verbs can show how likely or important something is.

7 I can use modal verbs in writing to show probability or importance.

1: Revising demonstrative determiners 1

Activity 1

Grammar guide

> We need **this** sugar, **these** eggs, **that** flour, **those** cake tins and **the** big bowl.
>
> We should also look for **a** wooden spoon and **any** cake decorations that you can find.

- **Determiners** begin both simple and expanded noun phrases.
- They can give information about whether something is **definite** or **indefinite**.

Underline all the definite determiners in the paragraph.

<u>Last</u> Saturday, I went to buy gifts for my family. I had a few ideas, but I hoped that trip would give me some inspiration. I knew I'd get these games my brother likes. I found this sweater with stripes for Dad and a new novel by my sister's favourite author. I got Mum those tools that she wanted. The day was really successful.

Activity 2

Grammar guide

> I got **these** posters for **this** wall and **those** posters for **that** wall.

- Demonstratives indicate nouns for definite things: things that are known.
- The four demonstratives are '**this**', '**that**', '**these**' and '**those**'.
- The demonstratives '**this**' and '**that**' indicate singular nouns, and '**these**' and '**those**' indicate plural nouns.
- The demonstratives '**this**' and '**these**' indicate items that are nearby, and '**that**' and '**those**' indicate items further away.

Underline the demonstrative determiner in each sentence.
Add ticks to show whether it indicates something 'indefinite' or 'definite', 'singular' or 'plural', and 'near' or 'far'.

1 <u>That</u> plant needs watering, please.
- ☐ indefinite   ☑ singular   ☐ near
- ☑ definite   ☐ plural   ☑ far

2 Would you like this banana?
- ☐ indefinite   ☐ singular   ☐ near
- ☐ definite   ☐ plural   ☐ far

3 You can take these gloves to keep warm.
- ☐ indefinite   ☐ singular   ☐ near
- ☐ definite   ☐ plural   ☐ far

4 Those birds go to the fountain every day.
- ☐ indefinite   ☐ singular   ☐ near
- ☐ definite   ☐ plural   ☐ far

Activity 3

Look again at the paragraph in Activity 1. Write the whole noun phrase that starts with each demonstrative determiner. Include any prepositional phrases and relative clauses.

1 that _____

2 these _____

3 this _____

4 those _____

2: Revising demonstrative determiners 2

Activity 1

> Add the suitable demonstrative determiner before each subject: 'this', 'that', 'these' or 'those'.

1. the books Maria put away   ____those____ workbooks
2. the chairs near me   _____ chairs
3. the picture over here   _____ picture
4. the hat on the peg by the door   _____ hat

Activity 2

> Write noun phrases that identify four things or groups of things that you can see.
>
> Begin each noun phrase with a demonstrative determiner, using each demonstrative determiner only once.

1. _____

_____

2. _____

_____

3. _____

_____

4. _____

_____

Activity 3

Add the correct demonstrative determiner to each sentence.

1 I wish I could see _____ mountains you visited.

2 Would you like to join _____ game we're playing?

3 We should note down _____ ideas we're discussing, before we forget them.

4 _____ day when we went to the beach seemed perfect.

3: Exploring demonstrative pronouns

Activity 1

This is an impressive sculpture, but I think **that** is the best artwork in the museum. The tourists have differing opinions: **these** agree with me about the painting, but **those** just ignored it.

- The demonstrative pronouns 'this' and 'that' indicate singular nouns, and 'these' and 'those' indicate plural nouns.
- The demonstrative pronouns 'this' and 'these' indicate items that are nearby, and 'that' and 'those' indicate items that are further away.

Write the suitable demonstrative pronoun for each subject.

1. tasks you are currently completing   _____these_____

2. a tree you see through a window   _____

3. a small injury to your hand   _____

4. activities you plan to do next week   _____

Activity 2

They **filmed** the sportsman as he beat the world record. Even **that** was exhausting!

- The **demonstratives** 'that' and 'this' can indicate more than noun phrases.
- They could indicate, for example, **actions**, ideas or a series of events.
- These could be expressed as **verbs**, sentences or sequences of sentences.

Underline the demonstrative pronoun in each paragraph. Note briefly what it indicates.

1 Most of the film we'd watched was just OK, but we did see the thief sprint across the rooftops, pursued by the police officer – <u>that</u> was exciting.

<u>the chase scene</u>

_____

2 Krissie handed me a note that said 'Mary was the one who betrayed you.' I told her that this was unbelievable. Mary would never turn against me.

_____

_____

3 Kamala looked at her family and friends, talking and laughing around her. She wondered if this was all it took to be really happy.

_____

_____

4 The truth was, Ray could have been in serious trouble if he hadn't left the street when he did – there was no getting away from that.

_____

_____

Activity 3

Imagine this sentence is the opening line in a story. Think about what the demonstrative pronoun may indicate, and write notes about why this could make an interesting first sentence.

I'd never before been as frightened as that.

_____

_____

_____

_____

4: Linking sentences with demonstrative pronouns

Activity 1

- The demonstrative pronouns 'that' and 'this' can indicate, for example, actions, ideas or a series of events.
- These could be expressed as verbs, sentences or sequences of sentences.
- Linking ideas across sentences like this can create cohesion in a text. Cohesion means the elements of a text work well together as a whole.

Note which demonstrative pronoun could replace each underlined phrase.

---

1 Freya watched as Cam flipped the skateboard in the air. 'You flipping the skateboard in the air looks great!' she called.

<u>That</u>

2 The laundry, the ironing, the cleaning, all these emails… With a sinking feeling, I realised that dealing with the laundry, ironing, cleaning and all these emails was going to take all day.

_____

3 We all knew that the headteacher's final suggestion would have a negative impact on pupils. The meeting felt useful despite our knowledge that the headteacher's final suggestion would have a negative impact on pupils.

_____

Activity 2

1 Write two sentences describing an idea that you have for a change to rules you have to follow, or tasks you have to do.

Start a third sentence with 'This', and explain why it is a good idea.

_____

_____

_____

2 Write two sentences describing something that you did last week.

Start a third sentence with the pronoun 'That', and explain how what you did made you feel.

_____

_____

_____

Activity 3

Underline one of the options as the second sentence in each paragraph, thinking about clarity of meaning.

1 April's plan was to get Mr Henderson to believe Maeve was cheating.

This was a ridiculous idea. / Maeve cheating was a ridiculous idea.

2 Sean was certain Apsara would tell her friends what had happened, or tell their teacher, or just laugh at him.

That was the worst thing she could do. / Telling her friends was the worst thing she could do.

What do I Know?

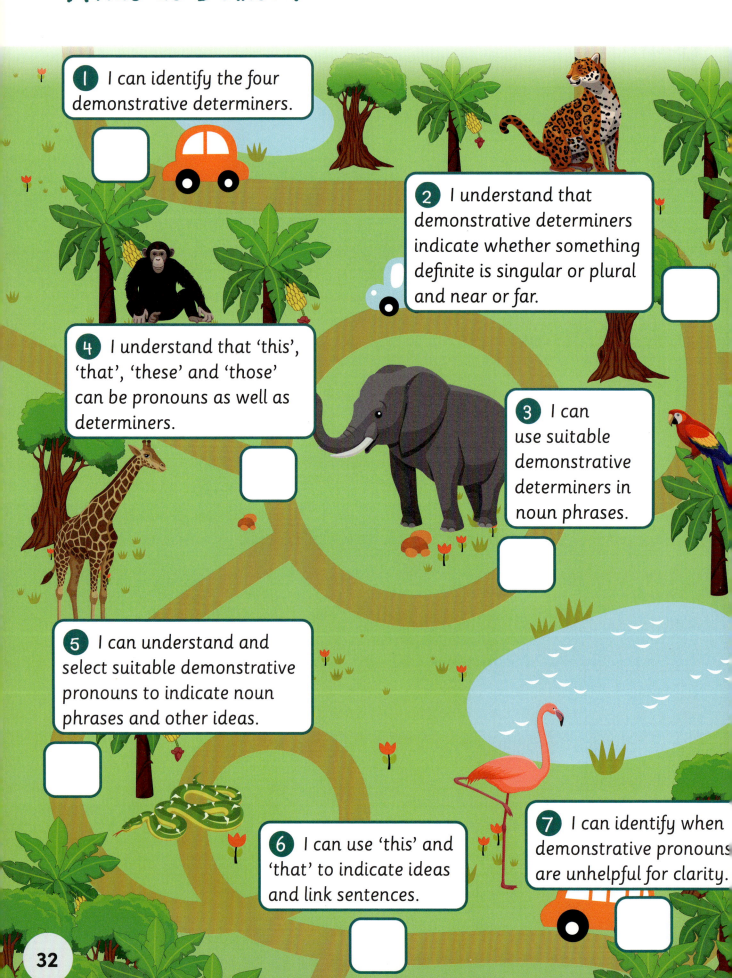

1 I can identify the four demonstrative determiners.

2 I understand that demonstrative determiners indicate whether something definite is singular or plural and near or far.

4 I understand that 'this', 'that', 'these' and 'those' can be pronouns as well as determiners.

3 I can use suitable demonstrative determiners in noun phrases.

5 I can understand and select suitable demonstrative pronouns to indicate noun phrases and other ideas.

6 I can use 'this' and 'that' to indicate ideas and link sentences.

7 I can identify when demonstrative pronouns are unhelpful for clarity.

1: What are relative pronouns?

Activity 1

Grammar guide

> the girl who is standing by the door

- A **relative pronoun** links a **noun or noun phrase** to **information related to it**.
- The following words are relative pronouns.
  - who   ○ whose   ○ whom   ○ that   ○ which   ○ when   ○ where

> Underline the relative pronouns.

Do you remember the time <u>when</u> we went to the seaside? We finally found the place where we were staying, but the woman whose cottage it was had left a key that didn't work! Thank goodness the neighbours who were nearby helped us: they found the man by whom the cottage was cleaned. He had a spare key, which he lent to us.

Activity 2

Grammar guide

> My sister is the **girl** <u>who</u> is standing by the door.
> This is the **boy** <u>whose</u> report you read in the school newspaper.
> That's the **teacher** to <u>whom</u> I gave my homework.
> Please pass me a **book** <u>that</u> is on the **shelf**, <u>which</u> is in the corner.
> I can't wait for the **moment** <u>when</u> I see you again, in the **garden** <u>where</u> we met.

- <u>Relative pronouns</u> can relate to a **person**, a **thing**, a **time** or a **place**.

Underline each relative pronoun. Note whether it relates to a person, thing, time or place.

1 The woman <u>whose</u> house is next door left us this note.

_____person_____

2 Callum had already eaten his pudding, which was delicious.

_____

3 The best part of the song is the point when the drums come in.

_____

4 The shop where we decided to meet is closed.

_____

5 Mrs Tyrell is meeting the politician to whom she sent her letter.

_____

6 The man who tutored Moira helped her do better at school.

_____

7 Mollie missed the hat that she had lost in the storm.

_____

Activity 3

Tick the sentence in each pair that uses a relative pronoun correctly.

1 Is this the person whom you wanted me to meet?

Is this the person that you wanted me to meet?

2 Isaac met a girl whose brother was in his class.

Isaac met a girl who's brother was in his class.

2: What are relative clauses?

Activity 1

Grammar guide

She looked forward to **the day** <u>when she could go home</u>.

- **Noun phrases** can be expanded using <u>relative clauses</u>.
- These are linked to the noun using a **relative pronoun**.

Underline the relative clause in each sentence.

1. The park <u>where we played as children</u> looks exactly the same.
2. This is Mr Reyes, to whom I passed on your application.
3. The path, which was flooded, was unsafe for pedestrians.

Activity 2

Grammar guide

Please look in the pen box: my pen is the one **that is red**.
This is my pen**, which is red**.

- A **definitive relative clause** adds information that is vital to meaning. In the first example above, we need to know the colour of the pen in order to identify it.
- The pronoun 'that' should be used for only definitive clauses.
- An **incidental relative clause** adds information that is not vital. In the second example sentence, the pen has already been identified when we learn its colour.
- The pronoun 'which' should be used for only incidental clauses.
- There should always be a **comma** before an incidental relative clause.

Tick the sentences that include definitive relative clauses.

- Tobi finally found the spot where she was going to meet Dad. ✓
- Mrs Cartwright is looking for the person whose bike this is. ☐
- Hari headed for the balcony, where it would be quieter. ☐
- This is the jumper that, as you can see, has a hole in it. ☐
- Connor introduced me to his aunt, who illustrates comics. ☐
- Erin turned up with a bunch of flowers, which were beautiful. ☐
- Which of you is the one who dropped that paint pot? ☐
- I'll meet you at eight o'clock, when I'll finally get into town. ☐

Activity 3

Tick the sentences that use definitive and incidental clauses correctly.

- Sofia was looking for her cat which has a green collar. ☐
- I remember the night the storm hit us when the lights cut out. ☐
- Sun and Tang finally had a long chat, which went well. ☐
- It was a shame, that we missed Sam's visit. ☐
- You've already been to my house, where we had the movie night. ☐

3: Selecting relative pronouns

Activity 1

Grammar guide

- The relative pronouns 'who', 'whose' and 'whom' relate to people.
  - 'Who' refers to someone who is the subject of a sentence.
  - 'Whose' relates to the owner of something in the relative clause.
  - 'Whom' refers to someone who is the object of a sentence.
- The relative pronouns 'which' and 'that' relate to things.
  - 'That' should be used for only definitive clauses.
  - 'Which' should be used for only incidental clauses. There should always be a comma before it.
  - 'That' and 'which' could be subjects or objects.
- The relative pronoun 'when' relates to a time. It is always an object in its sentence.
- The relative pronoun 'where' relates to a place. It is always an object in its sentence.

Select one of the following relative pronouns to complete each sentence. Use each word only once.

where   when   who   that   whose

1 It is the time of year _____when_____ shoots start to open.

2 Neil hadn't looked in the cupboard _____ Guy was hiding.

3 Freya and Anita, _____ had been chatting online, became good friends.

Activity 2

> Underline the correct relative pronoun in each sentence.

1. It was the clown at her first trip to the circus **where / <u>who</u>** had scared her most.

2. Around the corner came Paulo, **whom / whose** face she barely remembered.

3. Anjit wrote to the friends from **whom / who** he had received gifts.

4. That isn't the thing **when / that** I found most interesting.

5. Mia stared up at the sky, **that / which** was dotted with clouds.

6. The Morgan family would never forget the day **when / which** they left their old house.

7. The squirrel could not find the spot **where / who** it had buried its nuts.

Activity 3

> Select 'which' or 'that' to complete the paragraph, adding commas where needed.

Kerry had been out in the yard _____ was dusty and dry in the heat. During the last month, she had started planting the vegetable garden _____ she had been planning. Then there had been the drought _____ was entirely unexpected. "There are so many plants _____ will die without water," she thought sadly.

4: Adding relative clauses

Activity 1

Grammar guide

- Noun phrases can be expanded using relative clauses.
- These are linked to the noun using a relative pronoun.

Complete the sentences by selecting a relative pronoun and a suitable end to the relative clause. Draw lines to link your selections.

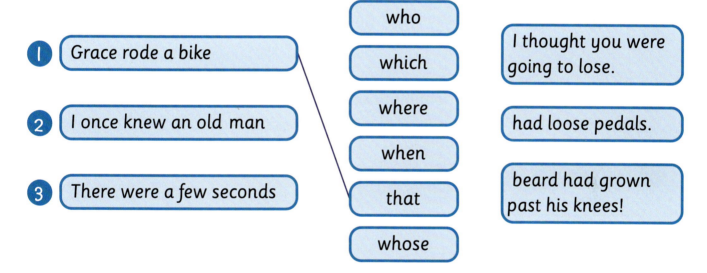

1. Grace rode a bike

2. I once knew an old man

3. There were a few seconds

who

which

where

when

that

whose

I thought you were going to lose.

had loose pedals.

beard had grown past his knees!

Activity 2

Grammar guide

- A definitive relative clause adds information that is vital to meaning.
- An incidental relative clause adds information that is not vital to meaning.
- If a relative clause is incidental, there should be a comma before it.

Complete each relative clause, making sure it fits with the relative pronoun. Think about whether it is definitive or incidental.

1. Asa remembered clearly the time when __he first met Hallie.__

2. Quickly, Jonah grabbed a box that _____

   _____

3. We picnicked in a large meadow, where _____

   _____

4. On the corner, they saw a woman who _____

   _____

5. There's a new pupil in our class, whose _____

   _____

6. There was suddenly a deafening sound, which _____

   _____

7. Zachary was searching for the person to whom _____

   _____

Activity 3

1. Write a sentence about a view from a window, using an incidental relative clause.

   _____

2. Write a sentence about a person you know, using a definitive relative clause.

   _____

5: What are implied relative pronouns?

Activity 1

> Jalal missed **the taxi** **that we booked**.
>
> He missed **the taxi** <u>we booked</u>.

- **Noun phrases** can be expanded using **relative clauses**, which give related information about nouns.
- Some <u>definitive relative clauses</u> use 'implied' relative pronouns. This means the relative pronouns are left out of the relative clauses.
- Object pronouns can always be left out. This means that 'where', 'when' and 'whom', and any prepositions before them, can always be left out. Other pronouns could be objects, too.

Tick the sentences that include relative clauses.
Underline the relative clause in each of your ticked sentences.

- That was the day <u>we went hiking</u>. ✓
- Hamsters often exercise in their wheels. ☐
- Mae met up with a friend she knew at school. ☐
- The way you answered that question was interesting. ☐
- The statue was put up in 1912. ☐

Activity 2

Grammar guide

> Jalal ran after the taxi **that** **was** <u>driving away</u>.
>
> He ran after the taxi <u>driving away</u>.

- If **a pronoun that is the subject of a <u>relative clause</u>** is left out, **a form of the verb 'to be'** has to be left out, too.

Identify which relative pronoun is implied between the underlined words in each sentence.
Tick the two sentences in which the verb 'to be' is also implied.

1. Follow the <u>girl running</u> under the bridge!　　　　_____who_____　☑

2. Can we go back to the <u>place we</u> had your party?　_____　◻

3. Three o'clock is the <u>time tea</u> is served.　　　　_____　◻

4. Cory was sitting at the <u>desk by</u> the window.　　_____　◻

5. Tuesday was the <u>day CJ</u> had a dental check-up.　_____　◻

6. The <u>teacher Maxime</u> met was called Mr Kyle.　　_____　◻

Activity 3

Underline the two words in each sentence between which a relative pronoun is implied.

There were some photos Mum wanted for our family album. She asked the photographer to suggest a time she'd be free and a place we could all meet. The photographer seemed like someone we could trust to do a good job.

6: Using implied relative pronouns

Activity 1

- Some definitive relative clauses use 'implied' relative pronouns. This means the relative pronouns are left out of the clauses.
- Object pronouns can always be left out.
- If a subject pronoun is left out, a form of the verb 'to be' has to be left out, too.

Rewrite the sentences so that the relative pronouns are implied. In one sentence, you will also need to imply a form of the verb 'to be'.

1 Do you remember the place where we're planning to meet?

   Do you remember the place we're planning to meet?

2 For a long time, it was Remi who was leading the race.

   _____

3 Alisah is the only girl whom I know in my new school.

   _____

   _____

Activity 2

1 Tick the sentences that would keep the same meaning if their relative pronouns were implied. In one sentence, a form of the verb 'to be' would also be implied.

- It was extremely lucky that Rayne caught the ball. ✓
- I can leave the moment when the final bell rings. ☐
- It was a beautiful day, which pleased Coco. ☐
- Mollie thanked her brother, whose bike she'd borrowed. ☐
- Imre was the one who was keen to come outside. ☐

2 Rewrite the ticked sentences so that the relative pronouns are implied.

It was extremely lucky Rayne caught the ball.

_____

_____

_____

Activity 3

1 Write a sentence in which the relative pronoun 'that' is implied.

_____

2 Write a sentence in which the relative pronoun 'where' is implied.

_____

7: How can relative clauses combine sentences?

Activity 1

Grammar guide

- Noun phrases can be expanded using relative clauses.
- These are usually linked to the noun using a relative pronoun.

Underline the relative clause in each sentence.

1. Anthony, <u>who is my best friend</u>, lives next door.
2. The game, which will be available from July, can be downloaded free.
3. The plant that is by the window is growing tall.

Activity 2

Grammar guide

<u>My sister</u> is extremely tall. <u>My sister</u> loves diving.

My sister, **who is extremely tall,** loves diving.

- Two sentences about <u>the same subject</u> can be linked using a relative clause.
- The **less important information** can become **a relative clause** within the sentence stating the **key information**.
- If a relative clause is incidental, there should be a **comma** before it.
- If it appears in the middle of a sentence, there should also be a **comma** after it.

Underline the words that make up the main point in each sentence.
Write a new sentence that gives the other information.

1. <u>Owen</u>, whose hair is bright blue, <u>is captain of the swimming team</u>.

   Owen's hair is bright blue.

2. Our teacher, who also runs the coding club, is ill.

   _____

3. Dipen's locker, which needs clearing out, is where he leaves his bag.

   _____

4. Break time, when José could call his father, was in ten minutes.

   _____

Activity 3

Tick the sentences that use relative clauses correctly.
Circle the mistakes in the sentences you have not ticked.

- Mrs Tam, who had taught for over 20 years, was retiring. ☐

- Gillie's coat pocket, he thought he'd left his phone, was empty. ☐

- The fly that has flown inside, is buzzing against the window. ☐

- Dan's hearing aid, which was almost invisible, was essential at school. ☐

8: Combining sentences with relative clauses

Activity 1

Add a relative pronoun to complete each sentence in the following paragraph.

The next weekend, __when__ Vincent and Amélie were at their uncle's wedding, was gloriously sunny. Their hotel, _____ was near the wedding venue, was great. Their cousin, _____ hadn't seen them for years, would be coming too. However, something _____ they weren't expecting was about to ruin the day.

Activity 2

Grammar guide

- Two sentences about the same subject can be linked using a relative clause.
- The less important information can become a relative clause within the sentence stating the key information.
- If a relative clause is incidental, there should be a comma before it.
- If it appears in the middle of a sentence, there should also be a comma after it.

Use a relative clause to link the pairs of sentences, choosing which sentence in each pair to use as the main point.

1 Mrs Augello lives at number 17. Mrs Augello wears a purple headscarf.

Mrs Augello, who wears a purple headscarf, lives at number 17.

2. The security guard was terribly afraid of spiders. The security guard peered into the shadows.

_____

_____

3. This evening, I'll be at home. This evening, I'll be able to finish my book.

_____

_____

4. The lawn needed mowing. The lawn was dripping with dew.

_____

_____

5. The library is where the painting was hung. The library is where Mr and Mrs Stedman first met.

_____

_____

Activity 3

Look at each sentence that you have written in Activity 2. Explore using the other sentence option as the main point and consider how the focus and effect change as a result. Write two of the new sentences that you feel work the best.

_____

_____

_____

_____

What do I Know?

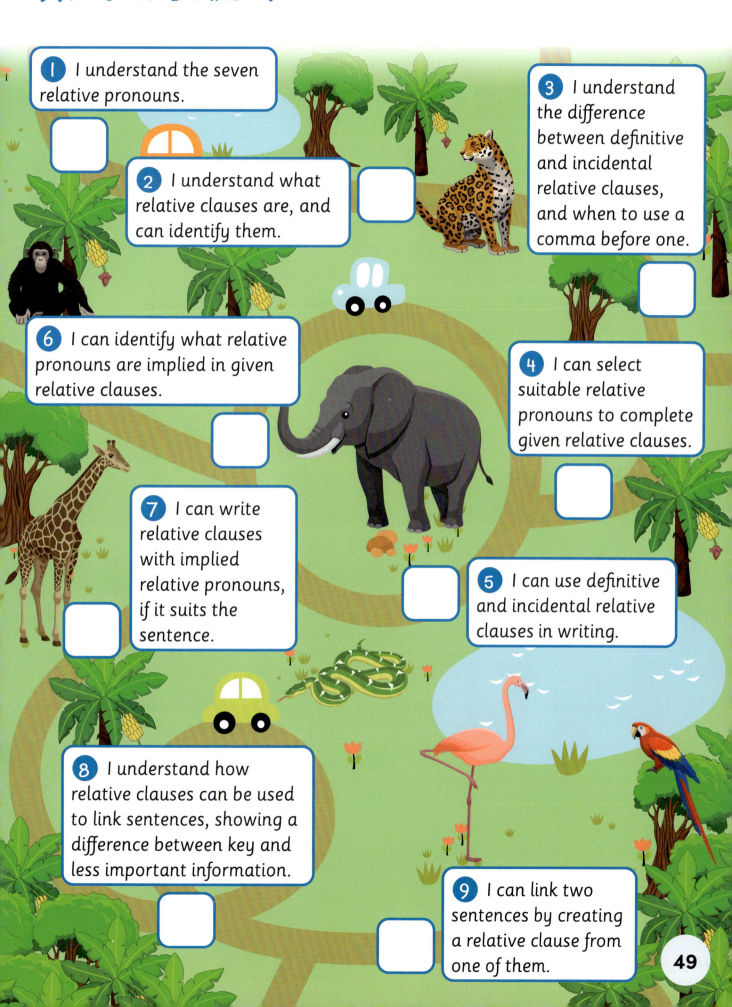

1   I understand the seven relative pronouns.

2   I understand what relative clauses are, and can identify them.

3   I understand the difference between definitive and incidental relative clauses, and when to use a comma before one.

6   I can identify what relative pronouns are implied in given relative clauses.

4   I can select suitable relative pronouns to complete given relative clauses.

7   I can write relative clauses with implied relative pronouns, if it suits the sentence.

5   I can use definitive and incidental relative clauses in writing.

8   I understand how relative clauses can be used to link sentences, showing a difference between key and less important information.

9   I can link two sentences by creating a relative clause from one of them.

49

1: Revising punctuation 1

Activity 1

Punctuation guide

> I have many hobbies. **For example,** I do swimming, drama, music **and** art, **which I love!**

- Commas should never be used instead of **end punctuation** to separate clauses.
- A **fronted adverbial** is always followed by a **comma**.
- Most items in a list are separated by **commas**. The final item is linked by '**and**' instead.
- An **incidental relative clause** always has a **comma** before it.

> Add upper-case letters and punctuation marks to the following sentences. The first two examples have been done for you.

W
we need eggs, cheese and butter

apparently we also need bread we

have run out which is surprising

Activity 2

Write a paragraph about going grocery shopping. Use:
- at least one list
- at least one fronted adverbial
- at least one incidental relative clause.

_____

_____

_____

_____

_____

_____

_____

_____

Activity 3

Look again at your answer to Activity 2, and check carefully that all your punctuation is correct. If there are any parts that need correcting, write the corrected versions below.

_____

_____

_____

_____

_____

2: Revising punctuation 2

Activity 1

Punctuation guide

> The **pupils'** new music teacher **hadn't** been at the school long.
>
> **"That's** Mr Han," said Inez. Then she added, **"He'll** be teaching us, **won't** he?"
>
> "He looks nice," replied **Inez's** friend, "so **I'm** glad!"

- **Contractions** are shortened words. Apostrophes show where letters are left out.
- The modal verb 'will' can be contracted to an apostrophe and 'll'.
- The contraction for 'will not' is irregular: 'won't'.
- A **singular possessive noun** uses an apostrophe and 's' to show belonging.
- **Plural possessive nouns that end 's'** do not take an extra 's'.
- Speech is enclosed within **speech marks**. Its identifier could come after it, before it or at a natural break within it. Exclamation marks and question marks after speech are kept, but full stops become commas if there is an identifier after speech.

Add capital letters and punctuation marks to the following sentences. The first two examples have been done for you.

M
my brother said, it wont be long until the prom

what is the dances theme this year I asked

I think he replied the pupils vote was for a

space theme

Activity 2

Dialogue is a conversation between two or more people, written as direct speech.

Write three lines of dialogue about a school event.

- Include at least three instances of speech, with the identifiers in different positions.
- Include at least one contraction.
- Include at least one singular possessive noun.
- Include at least one plural possessive noun.

Activity 3

Look again at your answer to Activity 2, and check carefully that all your punctuation is correct. If there are any parts that need correcting, write the corrected versions below.

3: What are parentheses?

Activity 1

Ivan's cat, **whose name was Socks,** slept in a basket.
Ivan's cat (**whose name was Socks**) slept in a basket.
Ivan's cat – **Socks** – slept in a basket.

- A **parenthesis** is a detail or comment that is not vital for meaning.
- Parentheses can be marked using pairs of **commas**, **brackets** or **dashes**.
- **Commas** create a less obvious separation than **brackets**. Writers can choose to use either, depending on how strongly they want to show that the information is less important.
- **Dashes** can be used instead, but only in casual everyday writing.

Underline the parenthesis in each sentence.

The Bulls – <u>our school football team</u> – played yesterday. We had (yet again) lost the match. Then Mikey, who's a great player, said he was quitting. We need – now more than ever – to train harder.

Activity 2

Suddenly, the window slammed shut.
A: Suddenly, to my surprise, the window slammed shut.
B: Suddenly (to my surprise), the window slammed shut.
C: Suddenly – what a surprise! – the window slammed shut.
D: Suddenly, the window slammed shut. (**This surprised me.**)

A: If there is already a **comma** where parenthesis is added in commas, only **one extra comma** is used.

B: If there is a **comma** where parenthesis is added in brackets, it goes after the closing bracket.

C: If there is a **comma** where parenthesis is added in dashes, it is removed.

C: Parentheses in brackets or dashes could include **question or exclamation marks**.

D: A **whole sentence** could be a parenthesis, placed separately inside brackets. Its end punctuation should be inside the brackets.

Tick the sentences that include correctly punctuated parentheses.

- That explanation, although badly expressed, makes sense. ✓
- Question 19 completely baffled me. (Did you understand that one)? ☐
- The ball crashed into – and completely smashed – Mr Todd's window. ☐
- If it was Sam who broke the desk (and I'm sure it was), he should own up. ☐
- Mr Wood, who's running for mayor is popular with everyone. ☐
- I wasn't paying attention and like a fool – walked right into the door! ☐
- The award (who'd have guessed?) went to Irina. ☐

Activity 3

Think about how the effect of the sentence below changes when different punctuation is used for the parenthesis. Note down your ideas.

| I will, maybe, win. | I will – maybe – win. | I will (maybe) win. |

_____

_____

_____

4: Adding parentheses

Activity 1

Punctuation guide

- A parenthesis is a detail or comment that is not vital for meaning.
- Parentheses can be marked using commas, brackets or dashes.
- Commas create a less-obvious separation than brackets.
- Dashes can be used only in casual everyday writing.

> Add commas, dashes or brackets around each parenthesis. Not including the example, use each type of punctuation only once.

1 Our teacher _(_ whose name is Mrs White _)_ is fierce.

2 It is __ finally __ Friday.

3 That book __ the one you lent to me __ was great.

4 Yulia __ unbelievably __ beat me!

Activity 2

> Add new information to each sentence as a parenthesis. Use a different kind of punctuation mark in each sentence.

1 The forest behind the houses was dark.

The forest behind the houses (which _____

2 It's OK to take snacks on the bus trip.

_____

3 They ran through the bushes to the path that led home.

_____

_____

Activity 3

Punctuation guide

> I cheated (which was wrong). Then I lied about it – which was worse. I apologised too late, which didn't help.

- If a parenthesis comes at the end of a sentence, it could be enclosed in **brackets**, with the sentence's **end punctuation** outside them.
- Alternatively, a **dash** or a **comma** could come before the parenthesis. In this case, the parenthesis should not followed by another comma or dash, just the sentence's **end punctuation**.

Rewrite your answers to Activity 2, placing the parentheses at the ends of the sentences.

1 _____

2 _____

3 _____

5: How can commas help with clarity?

Activity 1

> ### Punctuation guide
>
> I like cooking flowers and books.
>
> I like cooking, flowers and books.
>
> - **Commas** can be used to prevent ambiguity: unclearness of meaning.
> - They can also completely change the meaning of a sentence.

> Tick the sentences with meanings that would change or be unclear without their commas.

- I met Mary, Jane and Tobi. ✓
- Dyson, thinks Traher, is a good friend. ☐
- Shauna went to the cinema, with her sister. ☐
- It's a bright night, light with stars. ☐
- The picture showed a wood, fence and fields. ☐

Activity 2

> Read the following pairs of sentences. Explain the difference between their meanings.

1 Let's eat, Grandma!   Let's eat Grandma!

In the first sentence, someone is talking to Grandma about

eating. In the second,

_____

2 | We had chocolate cake and grapes. | We had chocolate, cake and grapes.

_____

_____

_____

3 | I got in, quickly looking around me. | I got in quickly, looking around me.

_____

_____

_____

Activity 3

Read the following pairs of sentences. The commas make definitive information into incidental information. Explain how this affects meaning.

1 | Bananas from hot countries taste great. | Bananas, from hot countries, taste great.

_____

_____

_____

2 | This is my friend Tom. | This is my friend, Tom.

_____

_____

_____

6: Using commas for clarity

Activity 1

Punctuation guide

- Commas can be used to prevent ambiguity or change the meaning of a sentence.

Change the meaning of each sentence by adding a comma.

1. He performs, plays and dances in his spare time.
2. We had ice cream and strawberries.
3. Is it time they should wake up Dad?

Activity 2

Write two sentences for each phrase, one with a comma between the words and one without.

1. **answer honestly**

   You might not believe it but he wouldn't answer, honestly.

   I asked him not to lie but he wouldn't answer honestly.

2. **cousin Peta**

   _____

   _____

   _____

3 hurry Francis

_____

_____

_____

4 end sadly

_____

_____

_____

Activity 3

Write one sentence of your own that would have its meaning entirely changed by the addition or removal of one or more commas. Write it once with the comma or commas, and once without.

_____

_____

_____

_____

What do I Know?

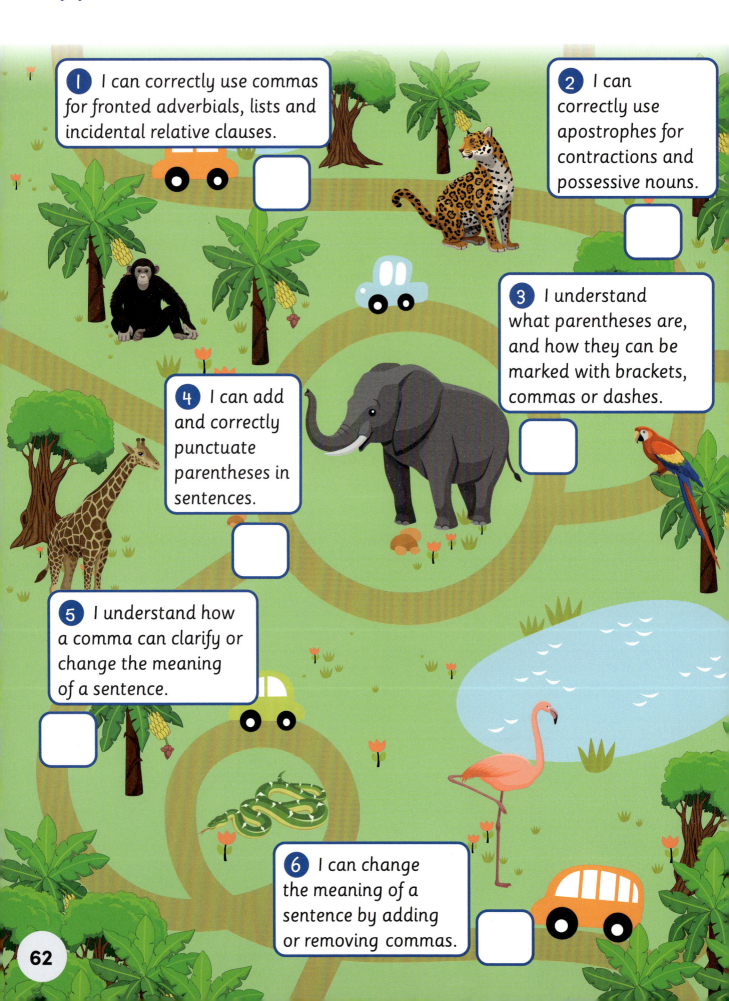

1 I can correctly use commas for fronted adverbials, lists and incidental relative clauses.

2 I can correctly use apostrophes for contractions and possessive nouns.

3 I understand what parentheses are, and how they can be marked with brackets, commas or dashes.

4 I can add and correctly punctuate parentheses in sentences.

5 I understand how a comma can clarify or change the meaning of a sentence.

6 I can change the meaning of a sentence by adding or removing commas.

Here are some useful meanings. Key terms to understand are in orange.

Term	Meaning
Absolute adjective	An adjective that could not have adverbials of degree such as 'more', 'very' or 'a bit' before it. For example: 'dead'; 'black'.
Adjective	A word that adds information to a noun. It describes what the thing named is like. For example: 'the <u>red</u> dress'.
Adverbial	A word (an adverb) or phrase that adds information to an adjective, verb or other adverb. Many adverbs end '–ly', but not all of them. For example: 'I ran <u>quickly</u>. I was tired <u>almost as soon as I started</u>.'
Agreement	The way in which all of the verb forms, nouns and other parts of a sentence match together in the right ways, such as in their tenses.
Alphabet	All the letters in order from A to Z. A list of words in alphabetical order starts with letters that come first in the alphabet. For example: 'apple, ball, cat …'.
Ambiguity	An unclearness of meaning. It relates to something that has more than one possible interpretation.
Apostrophe (')	A punctuation mark that can be used to show that letters have been missed out in a contraction or to show possession. For example: 'can't'; 'the horse's ears'.
Article	The words 'a', 'an', 'the' and 'some'. They are a type of determiner.
Attributive noun	Nouns that come before other nouns to affect and specify meaning, in a way similar to adjectives. However, they rarely describe what something is like but rather show what kind of thing it is, what it is for, where it is, what it is made from, or similar attributes. For example: '<u>car</u> park'; '<u>geography</u> teacher'.

Term	Meaning
Auxiliary verb	Verbs that are used to help create different forms of verbs. Forms of the auxiliary verb 'to be' are used in progressive tenses. Forms of the auxiliary verb 'to have' are used in perfect tenses. Within these verb forms, it is the auxiliary verb that changes to show tense and person.
Brackets ( )	Punctuation marks that are used in pairs. They are placed around text to indicate that it is a parenthesis.
Capital letter	Large versions of letters. They could also be formed differently from the smaller letters they match. A capital letter is used at the start of a sentence or a name. For example: 'A'; 'B'; 'C'.
Clause	A group of words, including a subject and a verb, that means one thing but is not a full sentence.
Cohesion	The way in which sentences in a piece of writing are linked together to become effective as a whole.
Colon (:)	A punctuation mark used to mark an introduction. It could introduce a reason, example, explanation or items in a list.
Comma (,)	A punctuation mark that separates items in a list and parts of a sentence that are not two clauses. It is often read as a short pause.
Command	A sentence that gives an instruction. Commands can be statements or exclamations, but they are never questions.
Compound	A word that is formed when two shorter words are joined together, with or without a hyphen. For example: super + man = superman; more + dangerous = more-dangerous.
Conjunction	Words that link together sentences to form one longer sentence. In the new sentence, the original sentences become known as clauses.
Consonant	Any letter that is not a vowel.

Term	Meaning
Contraction	Words that have been shortened. Apostrophes in contractions show where letters have been missed out.
Coordinating conjunction	A conjunction that links two main clauses in a sentence.
Dash (–)	A punctuation mark that looks like a long hyphen. Dashes can be placed around text in informal writing to indicate it is a parenthesis, or used in place of a colon or semicolon in informal writing.
Definite determiner	A determiner that indicates something known and specific.
Definitive	Detail that is vital to meaning (such as a definitive relative clause). For example: 'Please pass me only the pen <u>that is red</u>.'
Demonstrative	The four words 'this', 'that', 'these' and 'those'. They can give basic information about whether something is singular ('this' and 'that') or plural ('these' and 'those'), and nearby ('this' and 'these') or far away ('that' and 'those'). They can be used as determiners or as pronouns.
Determiner	Words, which include articles, that come before nouns. They can give basic information about whether something is singular or plural and definite or indefinite. For example: '<u>two</u> boxes'; '<u>all of the</u> things'.
Dialogue	A conversation between two or more people, particularly one recorded in writing.
Direct speech	Writing that reports exactly what someone says. A sentence that includes direct speech will include the precise spoken words in speech marks (or 'inverted commas') and often an identifier.
Exclamation	A sudden cry that shows surprise, excitement, shock or pain. It ends with an exclamation mark.
Exclamation mark (!)	A punctuation mark used at the end of a sentence, to show that the sentence is an exclamation.

Term	Meaning
Expanded noun phrase	A noun phrase that includes extra information about the thing named by the noun, for example using an adjective.
Fronted adverbial	An adverbial that comes at the start (front) of a sentence. It should be followed by a comma. For example: 'Suddenly, there was a crash.'
Full stop (.)	A punctuation mark used at the end of a sentence, to show that the sentence is a statement.
Future tense	A way of writing a verb to show that events or actions will happen in the future. It is formed by the modal auxiliary verb 'will' and an infinitive form without 'to'. For example: 'I will hurry.'
Future-perfect tense	A verb tense that shows that the action will have been completed before a particular time in the future. It is formed by the auxiliary verbs 'will have' and a past participle. For example: 'We will have watched the film before Friday.'
Future-progressive tense	A verb tense that shows an action that will continue over a period of time in the future. It is formed by the auxiliary verbs 'will be' and a present participle. For example: 'It will be raining all weekend.'
Heading	Words that appear as titles above pieces of writing. A heading tells the reader straight away what a piece of writing is about.
Hyphen (-)	A punctuation mark, which in form is like a short line. It joins words or parts of words together, to clarify meaning. For example: 'mother-in-law'; 're-cover'.
Identifier	A word that names the speaker of direct speech and includes a verb such as 'to say'. For example: "Hello," said Gunther.
Incidental	Detail (such as an incidental relative clause) that is not vital to meaning. For example: 'I've found my pen, which is red.'

Term	Meaning
Indefinite determiner	A determiner that indicates something general and non-specific.
Infinitive verb	The most basic form of a verb, preceded by 'to' (for example: 'to walk'; 'to be'). It expresses no tense and no person.
Inverted commas (" ", ' ')	Punctuation marks that show speech is being reported exactly. They are also known as speech marks. They can be double (" ") or single (' ').
Irregular	Words that do not follow rules when they change. Verbs could have irregular tenses. Nouns could have irregular plurals.
Letter	A symbol used for writing. One group of letters makes up one word.
List	A series of connected things. For example: 'In the pond, there are <u>fish, frogs, toads and newts</u>'.
Main clause	A clause that gives the main point in a sentence. There can be more than one main clause in a sentence if they are equally important. If there are two main clauses joined by a conjunction in a sentence, swapping the order of two main clauses does not affect the meaning of the sentence.
Meaning	The thing or idea that a word, expression or sign represents.
Modal verb	A type of auxiliary verb that suggests degrees of possibility, ability or obligation. For example: 'I <u>must</u> go.' 'I <u>should</u> go.' 'I <u>may</u> go.'
Noun	A word that names a person, thing, event or idea.
Noun phrase	A group of words that all link to the thing named by the noun. A noun phrase could be as short as two words: a determiner and the noun.
Object	The person or thing in a sentence that is not doing the action named in the sentence, but it is involved in the action. For example: 'Shanice plays the <u>game</u>.'

Term	Meaning
Paragraph	A clear section of a piece of writing, usually on the same topic. A new paragraph starts on a new line.
Parenthesis	A word, phrase or clause that has been added into a sentence as an explanation, aside or afterthought, but is not vital to meaning or the grammar of a sentence. It is marked by brackets, commas or dashes around it. For example: 'The wolf – a huge, slavering beast – prowled around the field.'
Past participle	A verb form used to form perfect tenses. A verb's past participle is usually the same as its past tense.
Past tense	A way of writing a verb to show that events or actions happened in the past.
Perfect tenses	Ways of writing a verb to show that an action is perfectly complete. They are formed with the auxiliary verb 'have', which is the verb that changes to show tense and person, and a past participle.
Person	The way in which a verb changes to show who or what does the action. Each person can be singular or plural. First person relates to oneself (for example: 'I'; 'we'). Second person relates to the direct recipient of a sentence (for example: 'you'). Third person relates to another person or thing named in the sentence (for example: 'she'; 'the cats').
Personal pronoun	Pronouns that represent grammatical persons. These include subject personal pronouns (for example: 'you'; 'they') and object personal pronouns (for example: 'me'; 'them').
Phrase	A group of words that means one thing but is not a full sentence. It could be as short as two words.
Plural	A noun or pronoun that names more than one of a thing, or a verb that shows that more than one person or thing is doing the action.
Possession	Something that belongs to someone or something else. This could mean it is owned by them or is related to them in a different way.

Term	Meaning
Possessive noun	A noun that shows possession. The noun for the owner takes the possessive form. For singular nouns and plurals that do not end '–s', this is made up of the noun, an apostrophe and 's'. For plural nouns that end '–s', it is made up of the noun and an apostrophe.
Possessive pronoun	A word that stands in for a possessive noun. Possessive pronouns can be determiners (for example: 'my'; 'your') or they can be used independently, to mean the possessive noun and the thing that is owned (for example: 'mine'; 'yours').
Prefix	A group of letters added at the start of a word to change its meaning. For example: <u>un</u>happy; <u>re</u>play.
Preposition	A word that makes links between parts of a sentence. It usually comes at the beginning of a prepositional phrase (for example: 'up the street'; 'around the bend'; 'with a big smile'; 'after lunch'). These can be parts of a noun phrase (for example: 'I live in <u>the house up the street</u>') or be adverbials (for example: 'I live <u>up the street</u>').
Present participle	A verb form ending '–ing'. Present participles are used to form progressive tenses.
Present tense	A way of writing a verb to show that events or actions happen now or happen regularly.
Progressive tenses	Ways of writing a verb to show that an action continues over a period of time. They are formed with the auxiliary verb 'is', which is the verb that changes to show tense and person, and a present participle.
Pronoun	A word that stands in for a noun or noun phrase. The words 'I', 'you' singular, 'he', 'she', 'it', 'we', 'you' plural and 'they' are all pronouns.
Punctuation	The marks made in writing that are not letters. Punctuation makes writing easier to understand.
Quantitative determiner	Determiners that give information about quantity. For example: 'all'; 'some'; 'every'; 'three'.

Term	Meaning
Question	A sentence used to ask for information. It ends with a question mark.
Question mark (?)	A punctuation mark used at the end of a sentence, in place of a full stop, to show that a sentence is a question.
Relative clause	A type of subordinate clause that is introduced by a relative pronoun. The clause adds extra detail, so acts like an adjective. For example: 'Flora, <u>who was an explorer</u>, set off for the jungle.'
Relative pronoun	A word that opens a relative clause by referring back to the noun or noun phrase that precedes it. The relative pronouns are 'who', 'whom', 'whose', 'which', 'that', 'where' and 'when'.
Root word	A simple word that could be altered by different prefixes or suffixes to form a word family. For example: 'farm' in 'farming'; 'please' in 'pleasant'.
Semicolon (;)	A punctuation mark used to separate two main clauses in a sentence if they are of equal importance. Semicolons can also be used to separate items in a list, if any of the items already contain punctuation (such as commas).
Sentence	A group of words that means one whole thing. It gives a whole idea.
Singular	• A noun that shows that there is only one thing or person. • A verb that shows that only one person or thing is doing the action.
Speech marks (" ", ' ')	Punctuation marks that show speech is being reported exactly. They are also known as inverted commas. They can be double (" ") or single (' ').
Standard English	English that is grammatically correct.
Statement	A sentence that ends with a full stop rather than a question mark or an exclamation mark. A statement gives a piece of information.
Sub-heading	Titles that are less important than the main title for a piece of writing. They appear before shorter sections and guide a reader through the piece of writing.

Term	Meaning
Subject	The person or thing doing the action. The subject carries out the action named by the verb.
Subordinate clause	A clause that gives extra information that is not the key point in a sentence. There cannot be a subordinate clause in a sentence without a main clause. If a main clause and a subordinate clause are joined by a conjunction in a sentence, swapping their positions affects the meaning or makes no sense.
Subordinating conjunction	A conjunction that links a main clause to a subordinate clause in a sentence.
Suffix	A letter or group of letters added at the end of a word to change its meaning. For example: farm<u>ing</u>; farm<u>er</u>.
Tense	The way in which a verb shows when the action happens.
Verb	A word that names an action. Every sentence must contain at least one verb.
Vowel	The letters 'a', 'e', 'i', 'o' and 'u'.
Word	A group of letters that make up one unit of meaning. In writing, a word has a space on each side of it. In slow speech, a word has a short silence on each side of it.
Word family	A group of words with the same root word and related spellings. For example: 'farm', 'farmer', 'farming' and 'farmed'; 'please', 'displeasing', 'pleasant' and 'pleasantries'.

Answer key

Exploring adverbials

1: Revising fronted adverbials

Activity 1
1. At the top [underlined]
2. After reaching ten [underlined]
3. If so [underlined]
4. However [underlined]

Activity 2
1a. time
1b. place
1c. cause
2a. number
2a. frequency
2c. degree

Activity 3
Firstly [circled] – number;
When I got there [circled] – time;
Consequently [circled] – cause;
Nervously [circled] – manner;
Just possibly [circled] – probability

2: Linking sentences with fronted adverbials

Activity 1
1. Later that morning,
2. Fortunately, though,
3. As a result,
4. At its edge,
5. Secondly,

Activity 2
1. Afterwards
2–5. [Children's answers will vary, but each must be a fronted adverbial that gives detail about:
2. place; 3. cause; 4. frequency; 5. degree.]

Activity 3
[Children's answers will vary, but each must be three sentences, two of which contain fronted adverbials that connect the sentences in different ways.]

3: How can fronted adverbials add structure?

Activity 1
However; Firstly; Secondly; Most importantly [each underlined]

Activity 2
[Sentences must be marked to form the following sequence.]
1a–b. Before you begin, make sure you have the correct kind of batteries. You will also need a small cross-head screwdriver.
2a. When you have your equipment, lay the remote control upside down.
3a–c. Firstly, open the battery panel by removing the two screws. Squeeze the yellow clip to loosen the panel when you have removed the screws. The panel is hinged and will open upwards.
4a–b. Next, lift out the old batteries. Dispose of the old batteries safely.
5a. Finally, insert the new batteries into the remote control.

Activity 3
[Children's answers will vary, but each should acknowledge that the fronted adverbials signal the flow of the text: a disagreement with the point in the first paragraph and three sections of supporting evidence, the third of which is the most important.]

4: Using fronted adverbials for structure

Activity 1
Marks should appear before each of the following phrases.
After lying in bed; Downstairs; All of a sudden; Running to the door

Activity 2
[Children's answers will vary, but each must use fronted adverbials to add different kinds of information.]

Activity 3
[Children's answers will vary, but should suggest alternative adverbials they could have used in Activity 2.]

Verb forms

1: Remembering tenses

Activity 1
1. Present progressive
2. Present perfect
3. Simple present
4. Past perfect
5. Simple past
6. Past progressive

Activity 2
1. wants; wanted; is wanting; was wanting; has wanted; had wanted
2. watches; watched; is watching; was watching; has watched; had watched
3. spies; spied; is spying; was spying; has spied; had spied
4. grows; grew; is growing; was growing; has grown; had grown
5. is; was; is being; was being; has been; had been
6. has; had; is having; was having; has had; had had

Activity 3
[Children's answers will vary, but each sentence must use a different tense.]

2: Perfect verbs for effect

Activity 1
1. being out in the rain; going home; being dry
2. practising; taking the exam; being relieved
[Children may use different verb forms or wordings, but comprehension of the actions/states must be correct.]

Activity 2
1. has lived
2. had run
3. had taken
4. has won
5. has chosen

Activity 3
I had bought eggs but I have broken them and now I need more.
I had felt unwell so I have taken the day off and now I feel better.
[Children's answers may vary in terms of conjunctions and adverbs, but the verb forms must be correct.]

3: What are future tenses?

Activity 1
I will be at home on Thursday evening. [ticked]
Mr Tirenz will do what he can to help you. [ticked]
They will look out for the helicopter. [ticked]
[All three instances of 'will' should be underlined.]

Activity 2

I will see you at school. [ticked]

be [underlined]

will really ['will' or space between words underlined]

We will have looked everywhere for these keys. [ticked]

It will be raining all weekend [ticked]

had [underlined]

Activity 3

1. future progressive
2. simple future
3. future perfect

4: Using future tenses

Activity 1

1. Nat will see me on Tuesday.
2. Daka and her sister will go home.
3. Uri will sing along with the radio.

Activity 2

Ideally, you will bring these instructions so you will be able to find your way. You will have caught the 11:30 bus from town. You will be getting off the bus when you will see the small park to the left. There will be a bright red postbox straight ahead. You will take the path by the postbox and there, to your right, will be my house.

Activity 3

1. will begin
2. will tell
3. will fall
4. will think

5: How are other modal verbs used?

Activity 1

should [underlined]; It should be easy for Mum to fix the blender. [ticked]

can [underlined]; I can come and collect the parcel after school. [ticked]

have to [underlined]; You have to get the train at 9:15. [ticked]

Could [underlined]; Could Jin-Yang come with us? [ticked]

Activity 2

1. third most likely
2. most likely
3. second most likely
4. least likely

Activity 3

1. obligation
2. permission
3. ability

6: Expressing probability

Activity 1

1. could
2. would
3. ought to
4. must

Activity 2

[Children's answers will vary, but each must be a paragraph that uses modal verbs to show a hierarchy of importance for the given events.]

Activity 3

[Children's answers will vary, but each must show the hierarchy of events used in Activity 2.]

Demonstratives

1: Revising demonstrative determiners 1

Activity 1

Last; my; that; these; this; those; The [each underlined]

Activity 2

1. That [underlined]; definite [ticked]; singular [ticked]; far [ticked]

2. this [underlined]; definite [ticked]; singular [ticked]; near [ticked]

3. these [underlined]; definite [ticked]; plural [ticked]; near [ticked]

4. Those [underlined]; definite [ticked]; plural [ticked]; far [ticked]

Activity 3

1. that trip

2. these games my brother likes

3. this sweater with stripes

4. those tools that she wanted

2: Revising demonstrative determiners 2

Activity 1

1. those

2. these

3. this

4. that

Activity 2

1–4. [Children's answers will vary, but each must be a noun phrase that includes a demonstrative determiner not used elsewhere in the activity.]

Activity 3

1. those

2. this

3. these

4. That

3: Exploring demonstrative pronouns

Activity 1

1. these

2. that

3. this

4. those

Activity 2

1. that [underlined]; the chase scene

2. this [underlined]; the idea that Mary betrayed them

3. this [underlined]; being among family and friends

4. that [underlined]; the fact that Ray could have been in trouble if he'd stayed the street

[Children may use different wordings, but comprehension of the concepts referenced must be correct.]

Activity 3

[Children's answers will vary, but each should acknowledge that the demonstrative pronoun indicates a frightening experience that is yet to be described.]

4: Linking sentences with demonstrative pronouns

Activity 1

1. That

2. this

3. that

Activity 2

1–2. [Children's answers will vary, but each should include a final sentence that uses the following demonstrative pronoun to refer to the idea/event described: 1. This; 2. That.]

Activity 3

1. Maeve cheating was a ridiculous idea. [underlined]
2. Telling her friends was the worst thing she could do. [underlined]

Relative clauses

1: What are relative pronouns?

Activity 1

when; where; whose; that; who; whom; which [each underlined]

Activity 2

1. whose [underlined]; person
2. which [underlined]; thing
3. when [underlined]; time
4. where [underlined]; place
5. whom [underlined]; person
6. who [underlined]; person
7. that [underlined]; thing

Activity 3

1. Is this the person whom you wanted me to meet? [ticked]
2. Isaac met a girl whose brother was in his class. [ticked]

2: What are relative clauses?

Activity 1

1. where we played as children [underlined]

2. to whom I passed on your application [underlined]
3. which was flooded [underlined]

Activity 2

Tobi finally found the spot where she was going to meet Dad. [ticked]
Mrs Cartwright is looking for the person whose bike this is. [ticked]
This is the jumper that, as you can see, has a hole in it. [ticked]
Which of you is the one who dropped that paint pot? [ticked]

Activity 3

Sun and Tang finally had a long chat, which went well. [ticked]
You've already been to my house, where we had the movie night. [ticked]

3: Selecting relative pronouns

Activity 1

1. when
2. where
3. who

Activity 2

1. who [underlined]
2. whose [underlined]
3. whom [underlined]
4. that [underlined]
5. which [underlined]
6. when [underlined]
7. where [underlined]

Activity 3

[comma] which; that; [comma] which; that

4: Adding relative clauses

Activity 1

1. Grace rode a bike – that – had loose pedals.
2. I once knew an old man – whose – beard had grown past his knees!
3. The were a few seconds – when – I thought you were going to lose.

Activity 2

1. he first met Hallie.

2–7. [Children's answers will vary, but each must end the relative clause with information that fits with the given relative pronoun.]

Activity 3

[Children's answers will vary, but each must include:

1. an incidental relative clause;
2. a definitive relative clause.]

5: What are implied relative pronouns?

Activity 1

we went hiking [underlined]; That was the day we went camping. [ticked]

she knew at school [underlined]; Mae met up with a friend she knew at school. [ticked]

you answered that question [underlined]; The way you answered that question was interesting. [ticked]

Activity 2

1. who [ticked]
2. where
3. when
4. that [ticked]
5. when
6. whom

Activity 3

photos Mum; time she'd; place we; someone we [each underlined]

6: Using implied relative pronouns

Activity 1

1. Do you remember the place we're planning to meet?
2. For a long time, it was Remi leading the race.
3. Alisah is the only girl I know in my new school.

Activity 2

1. It was extremely lucky that Rayne caught the ball. [ticked]
   I can leave the moment when the final bell rings. [ticked]
   Imre was the one who was keen to come outside. [ticked]
2. It was extremely lucky Rayne caught the ball.
   I can leave the moment the final bell rings.
   Imre was the one keen to come outside.

Activity 3

1–2. [Children's answers will vary, but each must contain a definitive relative clause in which the following relative pronoun is implied: 1. that; 2. where.]

7: How can relative clauses combine sentences?

Activity 1
1. who is my best friend [underlined]
2. which will be available from July [underlined]
3. that is by the window [underlined]

Activity 2
1. Owen is captain of the swimming team. [underlined]
   Owen's hair is bright blue.
2. Our teacher is ill. [underlined]
   Our teacher runs the coding club.
3. Dipen's locker is where he leaves his bag. [underlined]
   Dipen's locker needs clearing out.
4. Break time was in ten minutes. [underlined]
   José could call his father at break time.

Activity 3
Mrs Tam, who had taught for over 20 years, was retiring. [ticked]
pocket, he [space between words circled]
inside, is [comma circled]
Dan's hearing aid, which was almost invisible, was essential at school. [ticked]

8: Combining sentences with relative clauses

Activity 1
when; which; who; that

Activity 2
1. Mrs Augello, who wears a purple headscarf, lives at number 17.

2. The security guard, who peered into the shadows, was terribly afraid of spiders. / The security guard, who was terribly afraid of spiders, peered into the shadows.
3. This evening, when I'm at home, I'll be able to finish my book. / This evening, when I'll be able to finish my book, I'll be at home.
4. The lawn, which was dripping with dew, needed mowing. / The lawn, which needed mowing, was dripping with dew.
5. The library, where the painting was hung, is where Mr and Mrs Stedman first met. / The library, where Mr and Mrs Stedman first met, is where the painting was hung.

Activity 3
[Children's answers will vary, but each must rearrange the clauses in two of the sentences written for Activity 2.]

Punctuation

1: Revising punctuation 1

Activity 1
We need eggs, cheese and butter. Apparently, we also need bread. We have run out, which is surprising.

Activity 2
[Children's answers will vary, but each must be a paragraph that includes correct punctuation for at least one list, at least one fronted adverbial and at least one incidental relative clause.]

Activity 3

[Children's answers will vary, but each must correct any mistakes made in Activity 2.]

2: Revising punctuation 2

Activity 1

My brother said, "It won't be long until the prom."

"What is the dance's theme this year?" I asked.

"I think," he replied, "the pupils' vote was for a space theme."

Activity 2

[Children's answers will vary, but each must be a paragraph that includes correct punctuation for at least one contraction, at least one singular possessive noun, at least one plural possessive noun and at least three instances of speech, with the identifiers in different positions.]

Activity 3

[Children's answers will vary, but each must correct any mistakes made in Activity 2.]

3: What are parentheses?

Activity 1

our school football team; yet again; who's a great player; now more than ever [each underlined]

Activity 2

That explanation, although badly expressed, makes sense. [ticked]

The ball crashed into – and completely smashed – Mr Todd's window. [ticked]

If it was Sam who broke the desk (and I'm sure it was), he should own up. [ticked]

The award (who'd have guessed?) went to Irina. [ticked]

Activity 3

[Children's answers will vary, but each should acknowledge that the dashes are informal and/or that the brackets create more of a separation than the commas.]

4: Adding parentheses

Activity 1

1. ( )

2–4. [Children's answers will vary, but each must be a matching pair of brackets, dashes or commas not used elsewhere in the activity other than the Question 1 example. Question 2 is marginally best suited to commas, Question 3 to brackets and Question 4 to dashes.]

Activity 2

1. [Children's answers will vary, but each must complete the parenthesis appropriately, use a closing bracket at the end and follow it with the conclusion of the sentence: 'was dark.')

2–3. [Children's answers will vary, but each must add an appropriate parenthesis, one punctuated by a matching pair of dashes and the other by a matching pair of commas.]

Activity 3

1–3. [Children's answers will vary, but each must reposition and correctly punctuate the parenthesis completed in the equivalent Activity 2 question at the end of its sentence.]

5: How can commas help with clarity?

Activity 1

I met Mary, Jane and Tobi. [ticked]

Dyson, thinks Traher, is a good friend. [ticked]

It's a bright night, light with stars. [ticked]

The picture showed a wood, fence and fields. [ticked]

Activity 2

1. In the first sentence, someone Is talking to Grandma about eating. In the second, the person is suggesting that Grandma should be eaten.

2. In the first sentence, they had two things: cake and grapes. In the second, they had three things, including chocolate.

3. In the first sentence, looking around was quick. In the second, getting in was quick.

[Children's wordings will differ, but comprehension of each sentence must be correct.]

Activity 3

1. The first sentence suggests that only bananas from hot countries taste great. The second suggests that all bananas are grown in hot countries, and all taste great.

2. The first sentence suggests that Tom is one of several friends and has to be distinguished by name. The second suggests that Tom is the only friend present, so his name is not definitive.

[Children's wordings will differ, but comprehension of each sentence must be correct.]

6: Using commas for clarity

Activity 1

1. He performs, plays and dances in his spare time.

2. We had ice, cream and strawberries.

3. Is it time they should wake up, Dad?

Activity 2

1. You might not believe it but he wouldn't answer, honestly.
   I asked him not to lie but he wouldn't answer honestly.

2. [Children's responses will vary, but each should be two sentences, one of which suggests that Peta is one of several cousins and has to be distinguished by name and one of which suggests either that Peta is the only cousin, so his name is not definitive, or that Peta is being addressed directly by name.]

3. [Children's responses will vary, but each should be two sentences, one of which describes someone hurrying Francis and one of which addresses Francis directly by name.]

4. [Children's responses will vary, but each should be two sentences, one of which suggests that something has a sad ending and one of which expresses sadness at something ending.]

Activity 3

[Children's answers will vary, but each must be a sentence that relies on a comma, or lack of a comma, for meaning.]

My notes

My notes